D0816160

IN HIM WILL I TRUST

© Evangelical Sisterhood of Mary, 1995

ISBN 3-87209-648-6

Original title: *Vertrauensbüchlein*
First German edition 1993
First English edition 1995

Bible quotations are taken from the Revised Standard
Version of the Bible, copyrighted 1946 and 1952,
and used by permission.

Printed in Germany

In Him
Will I Trust

M. Basilea Schlink

Evangelical Sisterhood of Mary
Darmstadt-Eberstadt, Germany

Our soul
waits for the Lord...
Our heart is
glad in him,
because we
trust in his

holy name.

Psalm 33:20-21

No one

who puts
his trust
in the

LORD

will be
disappointed.

ONE LOOK AT JESUS

will
save us from
despair.

O Father, Father, I'm Your child.
What o-ver-whelm-ing joy is mine
To know my Fa-ther loves me!
He watch-es day and night o'er me,
Pro-vid-ing for my every need
With gra-cious lov-ing-kind-ness.

I sing and shout exultantly:
A child of God — oh, could there be
A greater, nobler blessing!
For me His heart beats lovingly.
My smallest cares He always sees,
My griefs and sorrows sharing.

TRUST GOD.
HE IS YOUR FATHER.
COME TO HIM
WITH THE UTMOST
CONFIDENCE AND SAY,

My Father knows all things,
can do all things,
and what He does is right.
My Father is good!
My Father loves me!

Those
who trust in
God's help
draw down
His help.

THE FATHER IS
GREATER THAN
EVERYTHING

God comes when all is dark.

He knows about your troubles and will help you.

He suffers with you.

He always knows the way for you to go.

He will never forsake you, for He loves you.

He is guiding you with a mighty hand.

Nothing can separate you from His love.

His help will not fail to come.

His power to help is greater than every hardship.

He will carry you through.

When you are at the end of your strength,
                    He will demonstrate His.

His angels are watching over you.

He has conquered your fear.

He knows how much you can endure.

You are in God's hands and not at the
                    mercy of people.

His will is nothing but loving-kindness.

When you are united with Him,
                    nothing can harm you.

His strength makes you strong.

Like a child,
confide in God
your father.
He will respond
and work in you.
HE WILL DO MORE
than you ask.

Do not throw away your confidence, which has a great reward. HEBREWS 10:35

A talk held in the Herald Chapel at Kanaan

This verse gives us a glimpse into the heart of God. Our trust is important to God — so much so that He promises a reward to those who do not throw away their trust. He knows how hard it is to keep on trusting during dark stretches in our lives. It does not come easily to us when our world seems to fall apart. Yet it is essential that we do trust in God in these critical times when troubles, doubts and sin are rampant and instability is increasing.

If we do not throw away our trust, we will find that we are royally independent of circumstances. We will be victorious amid all hardships, and Jesus will shine forth mightily in our lives. What used to get us down and at times threatened to overwhelm us, will fade into the background when we put our trust in the Lord, for trust carries a great promise with it.

> *Steadfast love surrounds him who trusts in*
> *the Lord.* Psalm 32:10

As we learn to trust in God, we will find that something happens. The following scripture, I am sure, will be familiar:

> *Daniel was taken up out of the den, and no*
> *kind of hurt was found upon him, because he*
> *had trusted in his God.* Daniel 6:23

Had Daniel failed to trust in God, he would have actually perished. If we do not experience help, often the reason is that we lack trust in God. Trust has tremendous inherent power. It can change everything.

Inwardly or outwardly we may be having a rough time. Perhaps we complain that nothing has changed in our situation, when in fact we may have been preventing God from intervening. He wants to help us. When the Bible speaks of trust being rewarded, this is not just a figure of speech: it is a reality. Moreover, this reward is not merely reserved for heaven. Here and now we will receive help if we trust in God.

On a human level, to what kind of person do I turn for help? It will be someone I love and who loves me, someone who has the power to help. If I have such a friend, then I am confident that he will really come to my aid. But who is the most trustworthy of all? In the whole wide world there is only one who is a hundred per cent reliable, and that is God. No one has such a capacity to love as our heavenly Father and no one can share our burdens as He does, for He is love. His love is beyond imagining. He cares about even the smallest details of our lives, and when we suffer, He draws near to us with His special love. Because God the Father has all power in heaven and on earth, He can do miracles, if we but trust in Him.

This we have seen in our sisterhood countless times. I can never praise God our Father enough for who He is. It is tremendous to experience His love and intervention in a seemingly hopeless situation, where there appears to be no way out. If God receives trust from us, then He stretches out His mighty arm and does wonders.

The fact that we are living here at Kanaan is a miracle in itself. As a young sisterhood, we had our first home in the Steinberg House, in Darmstadt, but then we had to move out with nowhere to go. It was just after World War II and our city had been destroyed by an extensive air-raid. Consequently, there was an acute

housing shortage. Then one day a sister visiting her parents came back with the wonderful news that her father wanted to donate us a small plot of land, where our Mother House now stands. The property on its own, however, was not enough, for what we needed was a house, as well as a chapel for our ministry. We continued praying, and the Lord gave us the scripture:

> Our help is in the name of the Lord, who made heaven and earth.   Psalm 124:8

There was great jubilation among us all. Now we had God's pledge that He would help us — the God who owns heaven and earth and who is Creator of all! He would do miracles and we would receive a home. Of course, we had no idea how, but He knew! With an initial capital of only 30 Marks we began to build with our own hands, using bricks we had salvaged from the ruins of Darmstadt. It was a challenging time, testing our physical and spiritual resources to the limit. All the glory goes to God for bringing the Mother House and Chapel into being, for 'our help is in the name of the Lord, who made heaven and earth'.

Our concept of God is often too small. *We* are small and insignificant, whereas He is great and almighty. He is the one who does miracles, and so the verse from the Letter to the Hebrews challenges us to trust Him when we can see no way out. It is as if our Heavenly Father were saying, *Am I not trustworthy? If a person is well-disposed towards you, you are confident that he will help you. Yet so often you fail to show the same trust in Me, although I am a God who works miracles.*

Some might say, 'You know, I did trust God in a particular situation, but no help came.' May I share with you a short prayer which has always helped me at such times:

> My Father, I do not understand You,
> but I trust in Your love.

It is true that at first we do not understand God when, in spite of our faith, no answer comes. This was my experience at a very dark moment in my life when it seemed as though God were going back on His word. At the time I wrote in my diary, 'My Father, I do not understand You, but I trust in Your love.' Years later I discovered why the Father did not answer my request: in His love He had a different and better plan for me.

It was a valuable lesson. Who am I? — Just an insignificant person, a mere nothing, a speck of dust. So how dare I say, 'If God doesn't do as I think and expect, I cannot trust in Him any longer!' How can I, who am nothing, comprehend the eternal God, who made the whole universe, the myriads of stars and all living creatures? He alone is great. This conclusion helped me so much back then that I said to myself, 'Who are you to think you can *understand* God? You need to *trust* Him. He is love. He will lead everything to a wonderful goal, if you are completely yielded to Him.'

When faced with overwhelming difficulties and tempted to give up, we will find it helpful to say: 'My Father, I don't understand what You are doing now and Your purpose in leading me through so many adversities. But even if I don't understand, I trust — and now comes the best part — in Your *love*. I don't just trust in Your almighty power, although that is wonderful enough, but I trust in Your love, which will never let me be tempted beyond my strength and which will always provide a way out.'

Looking back on a long life with various trials, I can testify to the reality of the scripture, 'God is love.' We just need to get to know this love for ourselves. He cares for us far more than we can ever imagine. When we are at our wits' end, He sees our plight, hears our cry and folds us in His arms. This is what is so precious about the words 'I trust in Your *love*.' If someone loves us, we can always trust him, for love seeks to help wherever possible. This is what our heavenly Father is like.

However, just thinking vaguely that we have to have more faith will get us nowhere. We need to declare war on everything contrary to trust: mistrust, unbelief, anxiety. Whenever a situation seems humanly hopeless, then I say, 'Begone, you demon! Jesus Christ has triumphed and unbelief — or whatever is keeping me from trusting — is vanquished!' It is a matter of putting up resistance. A trusting attitude comes from above, but anxiety comes from below and exhausts our inner resources. Thoughts keep whirling in our minds: 'There's no solution and I feel really depressed about my state. Things won't ever change.' From personal experience, I know that only if I immediately resist this anxiety or whatever is trying to get me down, can I be victorious.

We need to choose between two paths — trust and anxiety. Which path will we take? Merely discussing our troubles is not the solution. Action is required if we are to stop feeling discouraged and despairing of our situation.

We need to know how our anxiety can be defeated and how the spirit of faith and trust can triumph.

There is a little song which can help us here. It is simple but expressive of a childlike faith. Reminding the Lord again and again of our needs in song or prayer is effective, as we have discovered.

> I will trust You, O my Father;
> I'll believe and will not waver.
> For You, nothing is too hard.
> All anxiety will yield.

The last line can be altered to fit a particular situation. Such a song of faith is repulsive to the enemy and will drive him away. Then faith will bring forth its fruits.

However, this does not happen automatically. The verse from Hebrews 10 has to become a reality in our lives, as every scripture should. The decision is ours. Will I continue to walk in anxiety? Or will I now choose the way of trust? Whenever trust nearly dies away and worries rise up again, will I resist them in prayer or song?

Perhaps we think that transformation will come to us or a situation automatically. God has given human beings the freedom of will. If we do nothing and make no decisions, then nothing will happen. It is a matter of making up my mind. Will I continue to harbour worries, not realizing that a demon is behind my anxiety? Or will I begin to walk in trust? Will I say, 'Yes, I believe and firmly trust in God!' The enemy cannot bear that. He wants to destroy us. He wants to drive us to despair. But we are not going to allow this spirit of unbelief and mistrust to remain with us. It has no more right to us if we declare, 'I belong to my Lord Jesus. By His life He showed us how He trusted in the Father.' So let us choose this way and rededicate ourselves to the Lord, perhaps in words like these:

> This day I have decided
> not to throw away my trust
> but to honour and glorify You
> by trusting.

In your distress
say to God:

MY FATHER,
9 DO NOT
UNDERSTAND
YOU, BUT
9 TRUST IN
YOUR
LOVE.

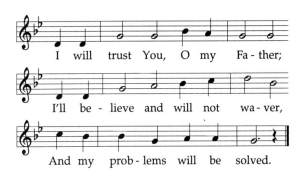

I will trust You, O my Father;
I'll believe and will not waver.
For You, nothing is too hard.

I will trust You, O my Father;
I'll believe and will not waver,
And anxiety will yield.

I will trust You, O my Father;
I'll believe and will not waver.
Unbelief will lose its grip.

I will trust You, O my Father;
I'll believe and will not waver,
And my fear will be dispelled.

I will trust You, O my Father;
I'll believe and will not waver,
Till my faith is hard as steel.

I will trust You, O my Father;
I'll believe and will not waver.
Everything will be transformed.

I will trust You, O my Father;
I'll believe and will not waver,
And redemption I will see.

I will trust You, O my Father;
I'll believe and will not waver,
For I know You'll bring me through.

I will trust You, O my Father;
I'll believe and will not waver,
Knowing You'll take care of me.

I will trust You, O my Father;
I'll believe and will not waver.
You will never fail Your child.

I will trust You, O my Father;
I'll believe and will not waver.
You will demonstrate Your might.

Pour out
your heart
to God your
Father.
HE understands
you better
than you do
and knows best
how to help
you.

TRUSTING WHEN WE DON'T UNDERSTAND

My Father, may the words 'God is love' be printed indelibly upon my heart.

Make me humble, so that I still trust in Your love in times of darkness when I cannot understand Your purpose in leading me along such difficult paths.

Help me to see clearly that as weak and sinful human beings we are limited and ignorant about many things. How can we understand You, the great and mighty God and Maker?

So help me in the coming times to say in dark moments:

My Father, I do not understand You,
but I trust in Your love.

I will put my trust in You, knowing that You will help me in wonderful ways.

And if I have to wait until You send help, You will give me patience and peace of mind and the sense of Your loving presence. Yes, You will give me the joyful assurance that You will bring me through in Your love, and that my love for You will help me to endure. For love is stronger than every hardship and attack of the enemy.

> I want to trust in Your love,
> O Father, Son and Holy Spirit.
> Nothing shall rob me of trust.
> I remain a child of Yours for ever.
> No matter how You should lead me,
> You have my consent,
> for I know that dedication to Your will
> prepares me for the heavenly glory.

Amen.

The angel
of the Lord
encamps around
those who fear him,
and delivers
them.

Psalm 34:7

Are you troubled
about the path
you have to follow?
Remember, God your
Father is leading you
in love. The path He
has chosen for you is
the best one of all.
Otherwise He would
have led you along a
different one.

We have
an almighty
Father in heaven.
Trust Him and you
will experience
miracles.

THE LORD
IS MY SHEPHERD,

I shall not want;
he makes me lie down in green pastures.
He leads me beside still waters;
he restores my soul.
He leads me in paths of righteousness
for his name's sake.
Even though I walk through the valley
of the shadow of death,
I fear no evil;

FOR THOU ART WITH ME;

thy rod and thy staff, they comfort me.
Thou preparest a table before me
in the presence of my enemies;
thou anointest my head with oil,
my cup overflows.
Surely goodness and mercy
shall follow me all the days of my life;
and I shall dwell
in the house of the Lord for ever.

Psalm 23

JESUS

has been given
all power in heaven
and on earth.
If we call upon Him,
He will conquer
all things for us,
even our fear.

THE POWER OF GOD IS SO GREAT

that He is always able to help you. He will direct your path.

Entrust yourself
to God, as a child
would entrust himself
to his father.
You will find that even
in the darkest
hour He will not let
you fall.

For God alone my soul waits in silence, for my hope is from him. He only is my rock and my salvation, my fortress; I shall not be shaken.

Psalm 62:5-6

My Father,

I can trust You, for You are nothing but love and You will use Your power to help us. So I resolutely renounce all anxiety. I want to trust You as I wait upon You in prayer.

As a wise and loving father, You will help me in every difficult situation, though how and when is up to You, for You know best which path I should take. For me, it is enough to know that You will bring me through and that Your timing is always perfect. I will not be crushed by my trials but emerge refined and reflecting more of Your glory. Thank You for the promise in Your Word:

> *The Lord is on my side to help me.*
> Psalm 118:7

Begone, all anxiety and defeatism! I have a Father in heaven who helps those who trust in Him.   Amen.

God the Lord
has a wonderful

Outcome

prepared for you.
Only for this reason
does He lead you
through
darkness.

MAY I BE A TRUE CHILD OF YOURS

Loving Father,
May I be a true child of Yours, immediately rushing to You with my problems, knowing that I may come to my Father with every trouble. That is where I belong. You understand me as no one else can.

May I also prove that I am a true child of Yours, my Father, by being able to wait until You send help. I want firmly to trust that in Your good time You will help me, resolving difficulties and showing me kindness. How wonderful is the assurance: Greater than my plight, greater than my sin and bondage, is Your love, which compels You to help!

Loving Father,
I commit myself to endure in times of distress and to wait for Your moment to come. I know it will be a moment of great joy and glory for those who willingly undergo the refining process of waiting. Thank You for preparing such a wonderful outcome.   Amen.

In dark hours say,

My suffering will
come to an end.
Joy and
glory will
follow for
all eternity!

Such words have power
to transform your suffering.

Lo, I am
with you
always,
to the close
of the
age.

MATTHEW 28:20

Other Literature by M. Basilea Schlink

FATHER OF COMFORT   128 pages

'Every day it has just the message I need.' — 'I find an answer to everything in life in *Father of Comfort*.'

REALITIES — THE MIRACLES OF GOD EXPERIENCED TODAY   128 pages

(American edition: REALITIES OF FAITH)

A book which does not deal theoretically with the idea of a God who works miracles, but which is a factual report of what the living God has done.

STRONG IN THE TIME OF TESTING   96 pages

As Christians face growing pressures, the need to prepare for the testing of our faith is even more urgent than when these texts and prayers were originally written. As Mother Basilea encouragingly shares, in Jesus Christ we can find all the grace we need to stand the test of suffering.

MORE PRECIOUS THAN GOLD   192 pages

A word of comfort, a challenge or a promise for every day of the year. In God's rules for living lies the key to His blessing upon our family, community and nation.

NATURE OUT OF CONTROL? 96 pages

In view of the recent floods, fires, quakes and blizzards, people are beginning to ask, 'Is God trying to tell us something?' . . . The present age, characterized by turmoil in nature, is an opportunity to know the living God as never before.

BUILDING A WALL OF PRAYER 96 pages

An intercessor's handbook

Everyone who knows and loves the Lord — not just some special elite — can be an effective intercessor. Here we are told how.

I WILL FEAR NO EVIL

(12-page leaflet with colour photos)

An encouraging message on the Psalms.